BOY

LESSONS

BOY LESSONS

WHAT I'VE LEARNED FROM MY SONS

JEFF JOHNSON

Boy Lessons: What I've Learned from My Sons
© 2021 Jeff Johnson

Edited by Sarah Kolb-Williams and Marly Cornell
Cover Illustrations from Vecteezy.com

ISBN: 978-1-7359135-0-6
Printed in the United States of America
First Printing: 2021
25 24 23 22 21   5 4 3 2 1

To order, visit BoyLessons.org.

To Sondi, Thor, and Rolf

Contents

I'm a Dad.

I'm also a lot of other things, but my most important title is Dad. It will determine more than anything else my final self-evaluation in life. How my sons turn out will be my most impactful measure of success.

There are a multitude of books out there about what fathers should teach their sons. I've read some of them and tried as a dad to follow their advice. I'm not sure I was great at it, but I did my best. Hopefully my boys learned a lot from me—I know I learned a lot from them.

It's not that my sons have imparted a great deal of wisdom from their brains to mine, but raising kids teaches a parent a lot. And raising my sons has made me a better man.

I need to be up front right off the bat. I think I've been a pretty good dad, but far from great. In fact, many of the lessons I list in this book I learned because I failed as a dad. Some of the lessons I learned too late to benefit my sons.

For example, I have a very long anger fuse. It takes quite a bit to get me to lose my temper or yell at someone, but one of my sons had an impressive ability to trip that fuse. And every time I yelled at him, I walked away after and resolved not to do that again—and then I did.

In *The Second Mountain*, David Brooks makes a great point about authors: "Those of us who are writers work out our stuff in public, even under the guise of pretending to write about someone else. In other words, we try to teach what it is that we really need to learn . . . I've written this book, in part, to remind myself of the kind of life I want to live."

I can relate.

I've written this book to share stories, honor my wonderful family, and remind myself of the kind of dad I still want to be—because even though my boys are now young men, a dad can still teach and learn.

Let me tell you a little about my sons.

BOY LESSONS

At the time I write this, Thor is twenty-two and about to graduate from college with a degree in supply chain management. Rolf is nineteen and a sophomore in college with a plan to teach elementary school. As is often the case with siblings, we question how the same parents and genes could have created such different young men.

As a toddler, Thor fit his name (and his red hair) well—fiery, emotional, demanding. His daycare teachers called him General One Shoe (based on his habit of taking off one shoe and shaking it at other kids while he bossed them around). By contrast, Rolf in his earliest years was always cheerful, quiet, and very easygoing. Save for the breakdown-inducing colic he had as a baby, he was a picture-perfect little guy.

Somewhere in their late elementary years, however, things changed for our boys. Thor started to become more reserved, calm, and introspective. To this day he prefers a close group of friends to being the life of the party. He remains even keel, very kind, and fiercely loyal; he's certainly the healthiest and most physically active member of the Johnson family.

Rolf's personality developed as well. Still he always has a laugh to share, but he lost the title of our calm and quiet kid many years ago. He's outgoing, has a huge heart for people, and is much more emotional and sensitive than Thor. He's a big boy, about six foot four and 240; but he isn't an intimidator, more a big, goofy, fun-loving teddy bear. And he's as stubborn as a mule. On a really bad day. With a migraine.

Thor and Rolf grew up as typical boys, loving sports, friends, and the *social* aspects of school. Their grades were fine (mostly), but they could have been better with more effort. Like father, like son, I guess.

And they were definitely both "all boy," sometimes shocking their mother with their crass or vulgar behavior. My wife, Sondi, at times threatened them with something called "Cotillion"—a mixed-gender Miss Manners type of class for kids intended to teach them proper behavior. She told them if they didn't clean up their act, she'd send them there to learn fancy things like dancing and social etiquette. I always thought they could use help in more fundamental ways, like using utensils or farting more quietly. But they were always just smart enough to avoid that threatened nightmare.

Every boy has his moments (or days or years) when they are irritating, disappointing, and at times truly maddening. And any parent who suggests otherwise is lying. I questioned more than once how bad a dad I was because of something one of my boys said or did. And it's amazing over twenty years how many times in a single day you can go from unconditional and unchallenged feelings of pride and love to absolute exasperation.

Raising boys is exhausting, confusing, sometimes even infuriating . . . and absolutely awesome.

The most impactful lesson I learned from my sons is the last one I discuss in this book, but I'll preface it here: A son is the greatest earthly gift God gives. Even on the really bad days.

Trying to remember that and act accordingly is the greatest challenge of fatherhood.

Take Conversations
When They Come.

Some boys are more talkative with their parents than others, but I gather most of them go through a period in their teens when parental communication is pretty sparse.

That always bothered Sondi more than me—probably because I'm a guy. I don't generally choose to talk about all the aspects of my day or share my feelings as easily as she does.

Both of our boys were chatterboxes until sixth or seventh grade. I recall in elementary school getting a report from Rolf's teacher calling him "charismatic" in the classroom. We were pretty excited to have a charismatic son until our teacher conference, when we realized she was just telling us (in a kind way) that Rolf was disruptive in class because he wouldn't stop talking to his friends.

Rolf has always been more expressive than Thor, but he definitely became more guarded in middle school. Thor clammed up with us completely.

Their reliance on texting doesn't help. They lose the practice of conversation and, even worse, things like "K" and "Ya" are considered complete sentences.

So I learned, once the "quiet" years hit, you have to take the conversations when they come—on *their* timeline.

Unfortunately for us, our boys most liked to talk late at night. Once they started driving, they were required to get their homework done after school. Then they usually ended up at activities or with friends most evenings. They came home for bed when we told them to come home, seldom before.

I once read about parents with little kids: It seems unfair that the people who want to go to bed have to put the people to bed who don't want to go to bed.

Well, the more things change, the more they stay the same. Most teens who drive (or at least our two boys) struggle to get up in the morning and then stay up as late as you let them (and sometimes later). Our boys were always most interested in chatting after they got home at night—usually when I was quite ready to call it a day.

Honestly, a long conversation was often the *last* thing on my mind. It's one of the many examples where Sondi was a better parent than me. But I did try, and it often yielded information and a small connection that I wouldn't have otherwise had.

Take the conversations when they come—even if you're really tired.

God Prepares Us for Their Departure by Making Them Practically Unbearable Before They Go.

Like all boys, both of ours presented us with emotional and personality ups and downs over the years. But they had one thing in common: About six months before they each left for college, they became surly, ornery, and particularly self-centered.

I love my sons unconditionally, but those months were probably the most trying for me as a dad.

And it's funny, because I remember dropping off each of our boys at college and having my mind flooded on the long drive home with all the things

9

I would miss about them—coaching sports, movie nights, mission trips, and just hanging out.

Obviously, absence makes the heart grow fonder IMMEDIATELY, because I also recall that a few days prior to his college drop-off at Iowa State, I was ready to rent Thor a room at the Ames Super 8 and buy him a bus ticket to head down early.

The drive home after dropping kids off at college (or otherwise sending them off on their own) is pretty sad, but God prepares us for their departure by making them particularly difficult right before they fly the nest.

There's Never Enough Food in the House.

Boys eat *a lot.* Maybe girls do too, but I can only share what I know firsthand. I didn't really understand it to the full extent until they were teenagers. And then came high school.

Throw on top that they're constantly eating huge quantities of everything while simultaneously complaining that there's nothing to eat in the house.

When our boys left for college, we likely covered about half the cost of tuition in savings on milk, Pop-Tarts, and toilet paper.

And even worse, someone invented Grubhub, DoorDash, and Uber Eats. When our boys were home from college during the COVID shutdown, they went through a short period when they thought it was reasonable to order overpriced food for delivery every time they were hungry.

That period ended quickly once we caught on, but it didn't change the fact that boys will eat you out of house and home one way or another.

Save the Real Battles for Things That Matter.

As parents, we have to pick our battles. Finding that fine line between nagging about everything and focusing on what's truly worth a fight is not easy.

Sondi and I didn't always agree about what necessitated a battle, but we did concur on things like putting an effort in at school, treating others with respect, and being honest with us.

Unfortunately, sometimes . . . okay, frequently . . . I defaulted into argue/lecture mode with my boys about many other things that probably weren't worth the fight. Things like leaving toothpaste globs in the sink, saving boogers on the wall behind their headboards, wearing shorts in the winter. And I could go on . . . and on.

I recall a frequent disagreement with Thor as a kid about wearing his baseball cap backward. It drove me crazy (and yes, I know it shouldn't have). I eventually won that battle and to this day he wears his baseball cap the way it was designed to be worn. But I probably should have saved those little battles for something much more important.

And it turns out, old habits die hard.

Not that long ago, Thor was home from college for a weekend and I woke him up for church on Sunday morning. He was slow to get up (Sundays are notorious that way in our house). As we were rushing out the door—late for church again—Thor bounded up the stairs in a baseball cap (worn correctly, I might add).

I told him he couldn't wear a baseball cap to church—it was rude and disrespectful. And just like that, we both reverted to baseball cap battle mode like it was 2010 again.

Thor told me he hadn't showered and wouldn't go to church without a cap. I said he should have gotten up earlier. He said lots of other people would be wearing caps in church. I said I didn't care. He said, "Fine, I'll just stay home then," and he disappeared into his room. And Sondi and I left without him.

Within a minute of leaving the house, I said to Sondi, "I'm such an idiot. He actually wants to come to church with us, and I told him no."

Sondi texted Thor, and he joined us at church a few minutes late—in his baseball cap.

By the way, he was wrong. There were *not* a lot of other people wearing caps in church, but there was one—another boy I knew from high school ministry who is kind, bright, and has a deep and mature faith. Thor was in good company.

Pick your battles. And if you're prone to argue, be willing to back down (or at least negotiate) on the small stuff.

Believe Their Teachers— Most of the Time.

When I was a kid, most of us dreaded our parents receiving a complaint from a teacher. We knew it would mean trouble for us at home.

Times have changed.

It seems now, more often than not, when a teacher complains about a kid, the parents move into defense mode and become angry at the teacher. Based on my experience with my boys, that is probably the wrong response.

It doesn't mean that teachers are never wrong about our kids, or that lousy teachers don't exist. Our boys had great experiences with most of their teachers. Many of them were fantastic, but there were a few clunkers in the mix.

By and large, however, when a teacher had a complaint about one of our boys, they were right.

In particular, both of our boys had a terrible habit of forgetting to turn in their homework. This often included homework we knew they had completed. It still baffles me that someone would go through the work of completing an assignment and then not turn it in—even after being nagged endlessly about it. But teenage boy brains are weird.

We got used to our boys telling us they had turned something in but the teacher must have lost it or was so disorganized that they hadn't recorded it. Occasionally that proved to be true, but usually the completed assignment (if it had actually been completed) was later found crumpled up in the bottom of a backpack among melted Gummi Bears, mechanical pencil parts, and who knows what.

Give their teachers the benefit of the doubt until they've given you reason not to.

Other Kids Aren't as Perfect as We Think.

Kids are hard to raise. Just like we were, they can be self-centered, irrational, inconsiderate, and, by definition, immature. And even the best of them do things that embarrass or anger us as parents.

But there's always hope. Just talk to *any* other parent. Compared to their friends, your kids aren't so bad after all. And my boys frequently reminded me of this when I was nagging them about something.

Being able to honestly talk about your kids is one of the joys of having adult friends with whom you can share anything. For Sondi and me, it has been small groups in our church where we can safely

18

talk about kid things that we might not share with our neighbors or parents of our kids' school friends. And it's amazing—the most well-behaved kids in the most well-adjusted families are still self-centered and sometimes stupid.

I don't think it's *schadenfreude*, the German word for deriving pleasure from another person's (or parent's) misfortune, but it sure is comforting to hear that your kids' faults are really no more intense than other kids' faults.

I remember sharing a couple beers a few years ago with a friend who had a son who was a junior in high school. He was rightfully proud of his boy, who was both smart and entrepreneurial.

I'll admit, my friend's bragging got a little overbearing after hearing about the book his son had written and the fact that he was coding at a level that would likely make him a millionaire by age thirty. But after a few beers, he shared with me that his son was not just sloppy, but simply refused to practice even a basic level of personal hygiene. His body odor permeated their house, and he could generally smell him across the room. He "faked" showers and brushing his teeth to the level that they actually had him seeing a therapist. I realize that almost any normal middle school boy has some hygiene issues, but not nearly to this degree, and certainly not at seventeen.

I remember leaving that night, not with satisfaction that this perfect kid was so imperfect, but rather recognizing that God makes them all different and vulnerable in unique ways—sometimes ways we don't recognize.

I love talking to other parents (who are honest) about their kids. It helps me realize that, despite their faults, my boys are pretty awesome.

Oh, and if you're ever *really* concerned about your kids' behavior, spend a couple days at Disneyland and watch other people's children. You'll feel much better.

When Money Becomes Scarce, They Become More Frugal . . . So Make Money Scarce.

Here's one where I wish I had a do-over. I don't believe we spoiled our kids. They certainly didn't get all of the things some of their friends had, but we live a comfortable life in a comfortable neighborhood. Our sons reaped the benefit of that. They were never really wanting for anything important.

I tried to teach them frugality through words and actions (some would argue I'm cheap), but I don't think kids really get it until they have to.

21

I realized that with Rolf on mission trips—the sheer joy in something that was normally taken for granted: a candy bar in the Boundary Waters; a lukewarm shower in Bolivia.

And I definitely noticed it with Thor once he was in college. As an example, he was home last summer and heading to a friend's cabin for the weekend. Included in his packing was a case of Keystone Ice. I asked him if he actually liked Keystone, and he said, "Well, I got thirty of them for $12.99, so yeah, I like Keystone."

They become frugal when they have to. And if I could do it again, I would have forced more frugality on them as kids.

There's an Invisible Force Field Around the Clothes Hamper.

Both boys had a hamper in their room for dirty clothes, and there was another one in the bathroom. Despite constant nagging, few articles of clothing ever made it in. Oftentimes socks or underwear were on the floor literally six inches from the hamper, as though they were desperately trying to make it in but fell just short, like a dying man crawling through the desert sand and collapsing just short of the oasis.

There came a point when we just stopped washing their clothes that didn't make it in the hamper. Unfortunately, our ingenious plan backfired. Our boys just wore whatever smelly, wrinkled, dirty clothes they could find once the clean stuff disappeared.

We never really solved this one. I eventually gave up, choosing to follow my own advice about picking the battles that really matter.

Enjoy the Little Moments.

There are big, memorable events in life with your kids that you will remember forever. Many of mine were part of either a family vacation or a mission trip we took together—significant impactful experiences we shared.

But sometimes it's the small moments together that are the most lasting.

With Thor, we have some of our fondest memories just watching football together on Saturdays and Sundays in the fall. I have some of those same memories with my own dad on Sundays sitting behind TV trays with Red Baron pizza and watching the Vikings.

And with Rolf, I remember in particular a camping trip the two of us took with Cub Scouts for a night when he was in elementary school. I'm not much of a camper, and the overall sleeping experience was miserable. It was hot and humid, the mosquitoes were swarming, the ground under our little tent was rocky and unforgiving, and we were surrounded on all sides by other dads in tents whose every snore sounded like they were gasping for their last breath. All . . . night . . . long.

But before we went to sleep, Rolf and I talked in the glow of a flashlight for an hour or so. He asked me to tell him the three greatest moments of my life. I don't recall my answers, because I was busy anticipating his. And he didn't disappoint me.

The first was his maiden voyage on a *real* rollercoaster. The second had something to do with a vacation we had taken in Florida. And the third: "This here right now—just you and me camping together."

Enjoy each little moment. It might just be one of the three greatest things your kid has ever done.

Spankings Are a Last Resort, But They Work.

To say we used spankings sparingly on our boys would be an understatement. Between Thor and Rolf, they received a total of one spanking—but that one spanking worked.

When Thor was in kindergarten, he was coming home regularly with "yellow cards" signaling he was being disruptive or otherwise naughty in class. He had a wonderful teacher who he loved, but we were still in the God of Thunder/General One Shoe era of Thor back then, and he was attracted to mischievousness like a duck to water.

After many discussions, scoldings, and time-outs, I used the ultimate threat: a spanking, if he came home with another yellow card. The threat worked—for about two weeks.

When he came home again with a yellow card, I gave him another warning (because I'm a softy).

But the day of reckoning eventually came. And when it did, I put him over my knee, told him this would hurt me more than him (which, of course, wasn't true at all), and gave him a solid whack. He let out a little yelp and turned his head back with a look of utter shock, obviously surprised that I actually followed through. He got a few more swats, and that was that.

He never had another yellow card again.

I probably should have used a spanking here or there again afterward with my boys, but the necessity when they were at an appropriate age never really presented itself.

Spankings work—at least in my limited experience. I'm not talking about belts or paddles or bruises, just a few stinging swats.

I realize some people may read this in horror and think I'm guilty of child abuse. Everyone is entitled to his or her opinion. But I was spanked (twice) as a kid, and it didn't scar me psychologically. It did, however, alter my behavior.

Likewise, Thor's one spanking was effective. So when time-outs become meaningless, and there's nothing left to take away from your kids, remember you have one more tool to use sparingly in your Dad toolbelt.

You Don't Have to Be Good at a Sport to Coach It.

When my boys were young, I helped coach them on a total of four soccer teams and six baseball and football teams. I didn't play any of those sports in school, and to be honest, I wasn't very good at them.

It all started with soccer—a sport I never played at all and one that still bores me to tears. But when they're five and no other parent wants to coach . . .

And at that age, soccer coaching is all about telling the kids which direction to run—and snacks. I was good at that. And thus began twelve years of showing up at every practice and game and "coaching," usually alongside someone who actually knew what he was doing.

Yes, there were downsides, like that godawful first year of kid-pitch baseball, but it was some of the most awesome time I spent with my boys—getting to know them better and getting to know their friends.

Dads (and moms), don't be intimidated to coach your kids when they're young because you don't know a sport. Learn just enough to stay one step ahead of them, and when they start getting pretty good, retire from coaching, knowing you've probably spent a few hundred hours with your child that you otherwise wouldn't have had.

Sometimes They Just Need a Mom.

There are many single dads out there who are doing a heroic job with their kids under difficult circumstances. I marvel at how well they often do and how hard their job must be.

My sons were lucky enough to grow up in a two-parent family, and I believe it was a benefit to them, because sometimes a boy just needs a mom.

There were times over the years where Sondi and I disagreed on parenting. Occasionally I felt she was too soft, too quick to forgive and forget, too accommodating when they were acting entitled or unreasonable. But on reflection, she always added the right touch to counter my (sometimes) rougher edges.

I remember the first break-up with a girlfriend in our house. They were fourteen years old (an age at which saying you're "dating" is a little silly in my humble opinion). It lasted for a few weeks, and she broke up with him in a text. He was devastated and I had little time for it—*they were fourteen*, for cripe's sake!

My response: "Get over it and move on."

His mom's response: "Talk to me about it as long as you want and we'll get through it together."

Her response was better, but not one that I could have pulled off.

Sometimes they just need a mom.

It's About *Quantity* Time,
Not Just *Quality* Time.

Back in the '80s, it was all the rage to promote "quality time" between parents and kids. It was a reference to time spent with your kids when you were able to give them your full attention, rather than being distracted by other things. The argument: It doesn't matter how much time you spend with your kids, as long as the interaction you have is "quality time."

There is certainly truth to the argument that quality time is important, but this trend also became a big cop-out for parents who spent very little time with their children.

Based on my experience with my boys, the quantity of time is as important as its quality—and probably more so.

The most enduring connections and lasting memories I made with my sons didn't occur because we spent an hour together occasionally in "quality time." Those connections were made from repeated and consistent time together, even if distractions were present.

The best examples I can give are coaching their youth sports teams, teaching confirmation, being involved in church high school ministry and mission trips, going on family vacations, and watching sports or playing games together.

Except for the family vacations, every example above involved activities with plenty of distraction; but because we did them over and over and over again, they yielded many opportunities to connect and bond.

Find ways to spend lots of time with your kids, even if distractions are present.

They Do Mature—Eventually.

There are days as a parent when you wonder if your kids will ever start "acting their age." Don't sweat it. They do—maybe just not as soon as you'd like.

For our boys, they went through phases that were each awesome in retrospect but sometimes pretty frustrating in real time.

Everyone's kids' phases are different, but this was our world (after the baby years):

Toddler/pre-K—mostly super-fun punctuated with massive temper tantrums and stubbornness. Also many memorable ridiculous events like melting the Comcast remote in the toaster and ending up in the ER after getting a crafting bead so far up his nose that it was practically scraping his eyeball ("It just fell in").

Early elementary years—a relatively sweet time when life starts getting crazy busy with kid activities and they start to worry and be anxious about things that shouldn't make them worried or anxious.

'Tween/early teen years—they love life in general—except for distractions like homework, classes, the basic responsibilities of life necessary to survive, etc.

Later teens/high school—they start to mature into young adults and gain a strong sense of independence (along with their driver's license). They also *finally* realize that God created the world to revolve specifically around them.

Post high school—real maturity, a budding appreciation for parents, and a pretty cool ability to have adult conversations with you that make you proud (minus the reversion to those high school years on their first summer back home from college).

There are many days over those years when you wonder whether they'll ever mature, but they all eventually do (at different rates). Enjoy each phase to its fullest.

A Boy's Love for His Brother Can Sometimes Be Hard to Spot—But It's There.

I didn't grow up with brothers, just one amazing sister with whom I still have a very special relationship. So my experience with how brothers interact is limited to watching my friends and my sons.

Brothers can be rough with each other. When Rolf was little, Thor mastered the art of making him cry (sometimes real tears and sometimes fake). He walked away each time with a look of supreme self-satisfaction.

Rolf in those toddler years always found less-direct ways to retaliate such as sneaking out of his bed one night to eat the gingerbread house Thor had painstakingly made for his grandma, throwing Thor's lucky cap off the Magic Kingdom train into the ditch-of-no-return, or loudly blaming Thor during sermons for Rolf's own silent church toots.

And later in life, this sibling rivalry was on glaring display when one got into serious trouble for doing something particularly stupid and the other turned into Eddie Haskell ("That's a beautiful scarf you're wearing, Mrs. Cleaver."), basking in the title of "good son" for as long as it would last.

Our boys could argue and bicker as expertly as any old married couple, but they also bonded with each other in many ways including a shared appreciation for the hilarity of belches, bodily functions, and any word related to those areas of the body that are supposed to remain covered.

In addition, they've always shown great pride in each other's accomplishments, encouraged each other in their challenges, and, more and more as they got older, chose to spend time with each other.

In many ways, they are as different as night and day, but it's obvious they will be best friends (and only occasionally mortal enemies) for the rest of their lives. It's a unique and wonderful bond I've seen between many sets of brothers.

If you have boys, let them fight. It will probably only strengthen their relationship as they grow older and begin to truly appreciate what they have in a brother.

Shoes Matter.

When I was in high school, I had my ASICS Tigers, a black-and-white pair of Vans, and boat shoes for when I needed to dress up. That was it. Boys didn't really care much about footwear in the '80s.

Times have changed.

Shoes are now important. In fact, I'm pretty certain our boys spent more on shoes than all of their other clothes combined. Thor was pretty much channeling Imelda Marcos for a while in high school.

It's even worse because they outgrow their sneakers in a matter of months, or they end up smelling so toxic that you have to leave them in the garage at night (the shoes, not the boys). And no, those ten-dollar sneaker balls don't make them smell happy and fresh.

Praise the Lord for Famous Footwear.

Teach Them How to Disagree.

I've always wanted my boys to question conventional wisdom and be willing to disagree out loud when they are disagreeing in their head. That doesn't mean being argumentative or disrespectful. It's very possible to disagree without being disagreeable.

Unfortunately, that doesn't come naturally for some people—especially teenagers.

I've been involved in government and politics since my kids were born, so they've been graced with (or subjected to) a lot of conversations about politics and policy, including a lot of disagreements.

They both have pretty deeply held views on important issues, although Thor has always been

41

more willing to share those views in the face of a hostile audience. I recall once when he was in high school, Thor was telling me about a debate they had in a government class about some divisive issue. He and a classmate disagreed, and his classmate laid out an argument for her case. Thor's response when asked by his teacher why he disagreed: "Because it's an idiotic position to take, and it's based on information that any intelligent person would know is false."

Thor was correct. His classmate's position was based on an assertion that was completely false and could have been dismantled with a five-minute Google search. But calling someone's position idiotic is not particularly effective in changing anyone's mind. And it certainly doesn't encourage others to listen to your position.

Teach your kids to speak up when they disagree, but also teach them to be prepared to explain their position before they speak up and to not make the disagreement personal. That's not the typical default of a teenage boy, but do your best to help make it the default for your kids.

They Need to Lose Sometimes.

Our boys were raised in the era of the "Everyone Gets a Trophy" rule. As long as kids participated (and even sometimes when they didn't), all were rewarded the same. There were often no winners or losers at all.

Thor has always been a good athlete, but he went through a phase of significant anxiety in elementary school. One of his friends convinced him to do a kids' triathlon in town one summer, and the requirements were not difficult for Thor's athletic abilities.

Unfortunately, during the swimming portion of the event, he had a little panic attack and was unable to finish his pool laps. He went on to complete the running and biking phases and then joined the other kids in the park for the awards ceremony where the organizers placed medals around each kid's neck with great fanfare.

Thor was not called forward for a medal because he didn't complete the event.

He was shocked. *Shocked!*

The concept of not getting the same medal as everyone else (as long as he had *tried*) was the very definition of injustice.

Letting little kids win sometimes is a good way to encourage them and boost their self-esteem, but they need to experience losing on occasion so they can understand that there are benefits to trying hard and outworking others. Shielding kids from any losses surely leaves them unprepared for success in real life where trophies are generally reserved for the winners.

Encourage Kids to Try Things That Scare Them.

Sometimes boys are irrational in their fears. For Rolf, clipping his fingernails was extremely traumatic for several years (think exorcism). And Thor (the Norse God of Thunder) was deathly afraid of thunder and lightning until he was almost ten.

Sometimes, you need to comfort and protect them from those little-boy fears until maturity and life experience help the irrationality pass. Other times, though, you need to encourage them, maybe even push them, to confront those fears and try new things that make them uncomfortable or scared.

45

Rolf was afraid of swimming as a young boy, and Thor wanted nothing to do with rollercoasters. Forcing those first swimming lessons was not fun, but we were there with Rolf throughout, and his fear was overcome, making for many great vacation memories over the years.

Thor fought us on rollercoasters as though his life depended on it, but we finally convinced him to ride with us (bribery is cheap when they're young). After that first terrified drop, there was no looking back. In fact, we were forced to put woodchips in the bottom of his sneakers more than once to meet height restrictions.

Don't scar them for life by forcing something on them too quickly, but encourage/push them to try new things that might make them nervous or scared. And be there to experience it with them. They'll thank you for it someday.

Sometimes It's Easier to Just Do It Yourself.

Some of us don't always delegate as well as we'd like—it's often easier to do something ourselves. That can be particularly true with kids.

I remember when each of our boys was learning cursive writing. It was excruciating to sit with them and watch them *slooooowly* write out a letter fifty times. The temptation to have them do five or ten and then finish the rest myself (in an appropriately sloppy manner) was intense. The same with helping them write papers in middle school. It would have been so much easier to get their input and then do it myself, but I fought that temptation. I knew it would have been beneficial for me but not so much for them.

Where I did fail here was with lawn mowing. I don't hate mowing my yard, but I could find a better way to spend ninety minutes on a sunny summer day. I looked forward for years to teaching my boys how to mow and have them take over that chore.

Unfortunately, it turns out, I can't really let go. My sons always did a serviceable job mowing, but not the way I would have. They didn't criss-cross the patterns correctly (or really at all). And don't get me started on edging around the landscaping.

On this one, I gave in eventually and just did it myself most of the time.

Was that all part of their brilliant plan? Possibly. Boys can be quite resourceful in devious little ways. But on the important things, bite the bullet, hunker in for the long haul, and make them do it themselves.

The Devil Does Some of His Best Work on Sunday Mornings.

To be even more specific, the devil does some of his best work *before church* on Sunday mornings. If you're a church-goer and you have kids, I probably need to say no more.

Sondi and I taught Sunday School throughout our kids' childhoods, so for years we got up early on Sundays to teach during the early service and then attend the late-morning service with the boys. There were some rough, harried mornings in that stretch. Once we got everyone into the car—almost always ten minutes later than I declared authoritatively the night before we'd be leaving—the boys would predictably start bickering. And just as predictably, Sondi or I responded with a frayed lack of patience.

Many times, the hangover of that drive extended into church when the boys argued about who would sit on the aisle and poke, elbow, and otherwise test each other during the quietest parts of the service (yes, even when we sat between them).

So, what God intended to be strengthening for our family as we prepared for and worshiped together was sometimes a bit of a disaster.

The devil's goal: make going to church so unpleasant and difficult that we eventually just quit trying.

Studies show families who worship together are stronger, and kids who worship with their parents (even if they're not paying much attention) are less likely to encounter certain problems in life. So don't give up. Power through those crabby mornings, and bring your kids to worship.

Know that the other families at church on Sunday, who seem to have it all put together, probably just went through the same thing you did.

They Might (Secretly) Listen to Your Music.

As our boys moved into their teenage years, the music they chose to hear became less and less enjoyable for me. I recall the same thing with my parents. They thought KISS was ridiculous when I was in sixth grade (which baffled me), and they thought GNR was downright subversive when I was in college.

But there is hope. Just as I quietly came to enjoy some of the music my dad listened to on his 8-track player (George Jones in particular), our boys secretly have a bunch of our music on their playlists.

I remember walking past one of my boys' rooms several years ago and hearing Foreigner playing (immediately transporting me to a junior high gym, standing along the wall, watching other people dance). Upon further investigation, I found they enjoyed a lot of classic '80s music.

So now when I'm honoring my dad by listening to Tom T. Hall or Merle Haggard, my boys might be appreciating Mötley Crüe or Poison. They probably won't tell their friends, but it's nice to know a little bit of us eventually does rub off on them.

Prom Has Changed.

Everything in life is more complicated than it used to be but, where we live, prom has gone off the deep end. In particular, boys don't ask girls to prom through a phone call or hallway conversation anymore. No, there is now something called a promposal. The boy, or sometimes the girl, has to make the ask in some dramatic and creative way that is prime material for social media.

A friend told me last year that her son rented a white horse to ride up to a girl's house and ask her to prom. Read that sentence again and tell me the world hasn't gone crazy.

It's safe to say that if promposals had been the expectation in the 1980s, I would never have gone to prom.

And the pre-prom photos are now an afternoon-long event, akin to a wedding photo session.

The extent of prom for me was finding a ruffled shirt that matched my date's dress color, having my mom buy a wrist corsage (safety first), and saving $25 to pay for a nice dinner.

I'm proud of my sons. They combined for three proms between them and both put the effort in for a promposal (although without the flair of a white stallion) and happily engaged in the two-hour photo event.

I'm just glad I grew up in simpler times.

Birthday Parties Have Changed Too.

Birthday parties of old usually meant inviting five to ten other kids over to your house to play games in the yard, open a few presents, and eat some cake and ice cream. For some parents (and lots of kids), something that simple might seem very foreign today.

Many parents now rent out portions of bowling alleys, trampoline parks, movie theaters, fitness centers, and amusement parks for their kids' parties. If they run out of ideas, they can always use the low-end fallback for uncreative parents: Chuck E. Cheese—where kids eat pizza, play arcade games, and contract minor diseases in a huge ball pit.

The presents today are *much* better than we used to get as kids, but the value proposition for parents is still quite poor with costs for such parties often running in the hundreds of dollars.

We never got too carried away with our boys' parties, but they were still too complicated for my taste. After all, if their friends show up, they'll have fun whether it's a big production or not.

Don't Sweat Their Irrational Behavior.

When kids are little and play hide and seek, they often believe if they cover their own eyes, no one else can see them. It's cute for a little kid, but it's completely irrational.

As they grow a little older, that irrationality reveals itself in different ways, but it lingers throughout childhood.

Don't sweat it; kids are irrational.

Thor, for example, was absolutely fearless as a kid. He was willing to try almost anything and, like so many boys, took his life into his own hands on a daily basis.

Except he was absolutely terrified of thunder. And clowns. And riding It's a Small World at Disneyland.

Rolf had his own quirks. He always loved school (minus the homework), but he went through a months-long period in second grade, fighting us every morning when it was time for drop-off. He was genuinely distraught and refused to tell us why. It took awhile, but we finally figured out that it wasn't a schoolyard bully. It was the toilet paper in the bathrooms that was rough, cheap, and disintegrated in his hands at the slightest friction.

There were simple solutions, like doing your business before or after school, bringing a little baggie of his own TP, or (as I suggested) sucking it up and acting like a normal human being. But he was seven, and kids can be completely irrational.

It doesn't just apply to the early years either.

In high school, Thor was meticulous about his hygiene and clothes. He'd often shower multiple times a day and genuinely cared about how he looked. But his bedroom came straight out of an episode of *Hoarders*. He looked good but lived in squalor.

All of this eventually passes, but kids are irrational, each in their own bizarre and unique little ways. Don't fret; each irrationality will pass and they'll move on to a new quirk that will drive you crazy. Then one day, they'll be adults.

They're Capable of More Than They Believe.

Some kids are pretty confident about their abilities, but most have plenty of doubt about themselves and what they can accomplish. Our boys were ready to drop difficult classes more than once because they didn't think they could pass. In the end, they got through, always with a lot of parental encouragement and a mom who rode them like a rented mule.

We saw this with our boys many times.

Thor is athletic, but he's not much of a skater. When he was little, he was adamantly opposed to skating lessons, but we live in Minnesota . . .

The first lesson was at our local ice arena, and there were twenty or thirty little kids out on the ice with a few teenage instructors and a whole bunch of proud parents sitting in the stands, watching from above.

That first lesson was an unmitigated disaster for Thor. He would fall down and then struggle unsuccessfully for a minute or two just to get back up on his feet, his skates and hands slipping about on the ice like a cartoon character. Once finally up, he'd fall again seconds later, and the whole pathetic spectacle started over again.

His instructors didn't help, as they wanted him to learn to get up on his own. So all of these children were skating around as he flailed on the ice.

As a parent, that's difficult to watch for forty-five minutes, and it didn't help when I heard the father behind me whisper to his wife, "I'm sure glad I'm not *that* kid's dad."

The lesson finally came to an end and, mercifully, Thor finished the lesson standing up, taking a couple tiny slides forward before it was over.

I was embarrassed. He was thrilled. "I did it, Dad! Did you see me? I didn't think I could, but I did it!"

Sometimes the victories are small, but with your encouragement and patience, and sometimes your insistence, they'll learn they're capable of more than they believe.

Make a Family Event Out of Whatever You Can.

Once kids start their involvement in school activities and other extra-curricular programs, it becomes much harder to do things together as a family. We did our best to turn some non-family events into a family affair.

For twenty years, much of my non-family time was spent campaigning. Our boys grew up walking in parades, attending fundraisers, and working political conventions. Yes, there was always the risk, as little boys, that they'd end up on camera digging in their pants, but we (almost) always had fun. And at least we were together.

Regardless of your circumstances and schedules, turn whatever you can into a family event.

They Probably Don't Know How to Write a Check, Read a Map, or Change a Tire.

There are many things important to me in my youth that my boys will never experience or understand: mix tapes, floppy disks, encyclopedias, record stores, "The Star Spangled Banner" on TV at midnight.

There are a few things of old, however, that could be useful to our kids, and they won't learn them unless we teach them ourselves.

A few years ago, Thor needed a passport and went to the post office to do all the paperwork with a blank check from Sondi for payment. He was back home in an hour, needing another check because he wrote the wrong information in the wrong places when the time came to pay. In twenty years, no one had shown him how to write a check.

When Rolf was in high school, he got a flat tire in the driveway, and I asked him if he knew how to change it. He said, "We can do that? I thought you had to call AAA."

I'll admit, I hadn't changed a tire myself in a decade or so, but we got an opportunity to do it together that day.

There are *so* many things we want to teach our kids, but sometimes we forget about the most basic of them until they stare us in the face.

A Weekend in a Smelly Gym, on a Scorching Field, or in the Freezing Rain is Still a Great Weekend.

There are few better ways to spend a weekend than watching your kid play sports in a tournament for several hours on end. This applies to non-sports activities as well, but our experience was with baseball, basketball, soccer, and Ultimate Frisbee tournaments.

Our boys always played on community or club teams, so we never had the crazy expense or intensity of some "travel" programs. It was always pretty laid back and fun.

BOY LESSONS

Every season we were part of a new community of parents and kids, and the memories of some of those tournaments are lasting.

It was the last game of a fifth grade basketball tournament for Thor, and we were down a few points with less than a minute left. The boy Thor guarded stole the ball and turned to run down the court for an easy layup to ice the game. Thor gave chase as everyone was screaming at him to foul the kid before he got a shot up.

Thor's only option was to lunge forward and grab the back waistband of the kid's shorts. He did just that, and (along with his underwear) pulled them down to his knees as they both tumbled around on the hardwood. It was the only technical foul Thor ever got in basketball, but it was one for the ages.

Regardless of the surroundings or weather, there's not much better than a weekend of kid sports.

Every Boy Needs a Dog.

We have an English bulldog named Chester. He grew up with our boys and he is in his final years now. Chester is grumpy, stubborn, gassy, and adorable.

In some ways, he's like a teenage boy—he doesn't shower us with affection like some dogs do and can be downright disinterested at times, but his love for us is deep and real.

There's a special bond between a dog and a boy. Chester doesn't show much emotion anymore (he sometimes lifts up his head from the couch when I come home from work), but when the boys return from college, he's an excited little puppy again for a few minutes.

BOY LESSONS

Boys don't necessarily have the enthusiasm for poop patrol they claimed they would pre-dog, but it's a unique relationship that every boy should experience.

Who They Hang Out with Matters.

We've been lucky. Our boys each have a large group of friends, all of whom we like. Have there been bad influences here or there? Sure, but other parents might be saying the same thing about our boys.

In general, we love our boys' friends.

And that matters, because the kids they hang out with affect what they do and how they act. And it only takes one kid to sway the whole bunch.

My very first year of teaching church confirmation was a challenge. In addition to Thor, I had eleven other sixth grade boys in my group. They were awesome boys, but they were also a handful. In particular, one boy (we'll call him Joe) brought out the worst in even the sweetest of the other eleven, instigating a lot of giggling, bodily sounds, inappropriate comments, and disruptive boy behavior.

I mentioned to the confirmation director, after my first session with these boys, that they were going to be a challenge. She said she'd come and sit in with me the next week to help, but I assured her that wasn't necessary. I could control a group of young boys on my own, thank you very much.

That next week, I had a heart-to-heart with Joe before we all got together, and he agreed to better behave. And he did, until he let one rip that literally shook the walls and filled the room with a gas so noxious I felt faint.

Of course it was hilarious to everyone in the room but me, and it caused a cascade of hysteria that went from zero to sixty in about three seconds. A couple of the boys dramatically fell off their chairs and rolled on the floor. One started banging his head on the table, and another ran around in a circle, waving his arms in the air. In an instant, we went from confirmation class to *One Flew Over the Cuckoo's Nest*.

At that exact moment, the confirmation director walked in to make sure I had everything under control.

It only takes one.

They're Watching and Listening Even When We Don't Think So.

Kids often seem completely disinterested in what parents say or do, but they're often taking note.

As a dad, I know my boys are more likely to treat their mom with respect if I do. They're more likely to remain calm in a crisis if I do. They're more likely to pick up after themselves and help with housework if I do.

A few years ago, we were on vacation in Los Angeles and got stuck in really bad traffic. A shocker, I know.

We were trying to get to a Dodgers game. It was a ten-mile drive, and it took us over two hours. I had great seats for the four of us, but we found ourselves listening to the early innings on the radio as we inched along.

As the drive progressed, I got progressively angrier at the traffic around us and completely lost my patience whenever someone tried to nose in front of me, or when the car I was behind let multiple others "budge" in front of him while we sat still. And by the end of that drive from hell, I saw my boys doing the same thing from the back seat—lashing out at all the rotten drivers around us, something that was mostly out of character for them. They simply followed my example.

Kids also observe the other adults around them—not just you. When Thor was in second or third grade, we had a chance to attend Vikings training camp and spend a while on the sidelines with the players and coaches. It was an awesome time for both of us and, I learned later, a learning time for Thor. He had been paying close attention to a conversation between Randy Moss and Chris Hovan and learned several new special words that he proudly shared later in public.

Who says you need to go to school to get an education?

Whether it's our own kids or someone else's, always remember they're watching and learning.

Pray with Them.

If you're a person of faith, pray with your kids as often as you can. When our boys were little, we said a memorized prayer with them at bedtime.

Dear God, hear my evening prayer.

I thank you for your love and care.

I thank you for my happy day, home and friends, work and play.

Bless the ones I love tonight.

Keep us all till morning light.

Amen.

Once they hit elementary school, we skipped the rote prayer and gave our thanks and requests to God together each night. Sometimes it was hard for them.

Sometimes their prayers were a little silly. But sometimes mine probably are too.

It's so good for kids to be able to talk to God and not be embarrassed or self-conscious about it. And it's a wonderful few minutes to spend with your kid at the end of the day.

Praying with them gets harder as they get older and you're not putting them to bed anymore, but find a chance once in a while to be with them and God in conversation, even as they grow up.

Don't Make Idle Threats.

Part of being a parent is administering consequences when your kids deserve them. The problem: it's easy to threaten consequences but often quite difficult to follow through.

I've seen it many times in public places: an exasperated and angry mom or dad threatening all sorts of punishment to a kid who is acting up and embarrassing them in front of the world. And you know most of those threats will go unfulfilled, which means the next threats won't be all that threatening.

Timeouts for Thor in his toddler years could be pretty epic. If he was in a mood, I had to physically hold him in his little timeout chair until the consequences seemed real to him.

I can't be too smug here though. I know there were times when I threw a threat or two at my boys (usually a threat of losing something they valued) and didn't follow through because it would have been more of a punishment for me than them.

Taking the keys away, taking their phone away, grounding them for a week. They're all pretty painful for a parent because you're now stuck driving them around, or you're unable to get ahold of them, or you can't let them out of the house when their grumpy face would really look better somewhere else.

So be careful and wise. Threats come easy, but that screen time you just threatened to take away might be the only thing standing between you and insanity on any given day.

They Need a Family Outside Their Family.

My boys were both blessed to have a community of friends/supporters outside of their own immediate family. They went to a huge high school, so having a small close-knit group of people there (both kids and adults) was really important.

For Thor it was the high school football team. For Rolf it was Young Life.

Kids need a sense of belonging—both belonging to a group of people and belonging to something meaningful to them. They also need caring adults in their lives other than their parents.

Whether it's at school or elsewhere, make sure your children have another "family" to lean on in addition to you.

Grandparents > Parents.

Our boys were lucky enough to grow up with four grandparents. The relationship a grandchild has with his or her grandparent is pretty special and, in some ways, superior to the relationship with a parent.

Grandparents tell a lot of stories (some of which are true). They're almost never in a hurry to make a kid get out of bed, or get dressed, or get out the door. And they're *always* thrilled to see their grandchildren.

Plus, they seldom choose to discipline or correct behavior.

Our boys have had wonderful relationships with their grandparents. They've gone to the zoo, the fair, and the lake with them. They've golfed, fished, cooked, and had sleepovers with them. They've gotten to eat pie and Toaster Strudels as meals with them.

I'm in no rush to get old, but there is an odd little part of me that looks forward to the day when I can spoil my own boys' kids and then send them home.

Press the Pause Button
When Tempers Flare.

I'm very slow to anger, but my boys had a knack for setting me off. Nothing abusive or profane, but they could definitely get me going. And every time I yelled or overreacted, I promised myself I wouldn't do it again. And then I did.

I don't think I'm unique that way among dads.

It usually happened when I was trying to *calmly* correct their behavior, reprimand them, or share some unwelcome fatherly wisdom. They would interrupt me with excuses or a complaint about their victimhood, talking over the life-changing lesson I was trying to teach. I raised my voice. They raised theirs.

And we were off to the races.

I vividly remember a time when my boys were teenagers, and I lost my temper at both of them for something. I was hopping mad and they looked at each other and started to laugh. I thought my head would explode, but it reminded me of something I frequently told myself when the boys were little and particularly difficult: as the adult in the room, I should always act like the adult in the room.

As my boys got older, I got better at mentally hitting "pause" (literally seeing myself pushing a button) when it felt like things were about to take an angry turn. It usually worked, although I did learn that teenage boys, with some effort, can override a pause button . . .

We Learn from Them Even Before They're Born.

I was learning from my boys for months before they were born. They taught me to love Sondi even more than before, as your love somehow grows when your wife is pregnant. They taught me (the hard way) to assemble a crib *inside* the nursery, because it won't fit through the door after you've put it together.

And they taught me a new level of humility.

During our birthing classes with other expectant parents, we were all randomly given a word or term related to childbirth (dilating, contraction, etc.) and required to give an explanation of it to the group.

My topic: mucus plug. That's right, I got to give a little presentation to people I didn't know about the mucus plug.

Humility.

The actual birth experience was also instructive. Our boys were big (both about ten pounds). And Rolf's head was the size of a small cantaloupe. Neither labor was easy for Sondi, and the experience taught me a lot.

For example, our intense preparation and practice at "relaxation" and proper breathing techniques turned out to be unnecessary when the big day arrived. I learned this quickly by telling Sondi to "relax" once during labor. I didn't tell her again. I'm a quick study.

Boys Are Irresponsible.

Boys lose things. They don't turn in assignments and don't pay attention in class. They lose track of time, don't feed the dog, forget to check in with us, and break our stuff. They can be absentminded, careless, and clumsy.

Boys are irresponsible. It's how God made them.

But they do improve as they grow and eventually become responsible fathers who get to complain about their irresponsible sons.

When Rolf was a freshman in high school, he had some sort of "life skills" class. One activity in the course was to poke a pinhole in an uncooked egg and drain the contents. This hollow egg then became the student's "baby" for a week. Each kid was required to bring this fragile egg everywhere with them and protect it from harm.

Somehow, Rolf ended up with twins—two eggs to cherish and protect for seven days. On Day Three he lost one. On Day Six he sat on the other.

At fourteen, Rolf was too irresponsible to be a dad (or probably the primary caregiver of a turtle). Thankfully, he didn't need to be as responsible as a parent because he was a boy—and (to recap) boys are irresponsible.

One of the beautiful things about life is that boys become more responsible with each passing year. And when it comes time for them to be a dad, they're usually ready.

Social Media Distorts Their World.

I'm thankful we didn't have social media when I was young. I did a lot of stupid things in high school and college that would have been recorded for posterity rather than lost in the middle-aged memories of my friends.

Instagram, Snapchat, and to a lesser extent Facebook (which lost its luster with kids when young grandmothers started taking over in the 2010s) are seemingly omnipresent to this generation of kids. There is good and bad to that. They are able to learn and share and keep in contact on social media in a way that wasn't possible before.

Unfortunately, the negatives are pretty significant. Kids overshare both personal information and questionable images that can lead to problems for them years later. They're exposed to adult and offensive content on a regular basis. Their perception of reality and happiness is distorted as all of their friends are sharing picture-perfect posts about their beautiful selves and idyllic lives.

And of course, many kids believe they must have access to that little screen 24/7.

Worst of all, the *need* to have their pictures and posts "liked" by friends is intense. Constant and immediate affirmation on social media has become the greatest measure of love in some kids' lives.

This is an area where Sondi and I probably fell short as parents. Maybe it's because our boys weren't obsessed with social media or didn't have their phones in front of their faces all the time, but other than following them on Facebook and Instagram and installing a content filter on our home computer, we didn't really monitor their social media or internet usage as closely as we could have.

At this point, there are no signs that our boys' social media activity will come back to haunt them, but if I had a second chance, I'd try to find a way to balance better monitoring with their need for teenage privacy.

We Sometimes Measure Their Behavior with a Double Standard.

Sometimes when I find myself upset or angry with my boys, I stop to realize they're acting the same way I did as a kid. Whether it's big things or little, I sometimes have judged them with a double standard when compared to my younger self.

When Thor was little, it annoyed me that the mere smell of a green vegetable sent him into exaggerated bouts of incapacity. But my own dad later reminded me that I forced myself to throw up when I was required to eat peas as a little boy.

I remember my disgust with my boys in the year-end middle-school locker cleanout as we needed multiple layers of protective gear just to survive. And then I remembered my junior high locker . . .

I've lamented the fact that their effort in school wasn't always as robust as it should have been or that they made some unwise or even risky choices in their teenage years—all things to which the 1980s Jeff Johnson could maybe possibly conceivably have related.

Granted, there are certainly things they have done that I wouldn't have as a kid, but sometimes it's important to put things into perspective as a dad and realize they really do take after us—in good ways and bad.

Show Them Resilience.

Every kid's life is full of ups and downs. They can become discouraged easily, especially in the drama-filled teenage years.

They need to see their parents bounce back from trials and adversity, because (as we know) they often follow our lead.

This is less of an issue when they're little. I recall many elementary school baseball and soccer games when the boys were bummed about losing—for approximately five seconds. Then the snacks and juice boxes came out, and a bright new day dawned.

In their teenage years, losses become more painful and trials much more serious. Relationships, grades, jobs, and competitive sports and activities are all opportunities for disappointment and failure.

Let them know about your setbacks and defeats and how you picked yourself up each time. They'll rebound much better if we show them how it's done.

Teach Them to Give and Serve.

When our boys were young, I recall having a conversation with some friends about growing up in the Lutheran church. One friend told us that she had recently learned her parents tithed (contributed 10 percent of their income) to their church during her childhood. She was upset, arguing that they lived a rather austere life back then, and there could have been more money for the family had her parents not made that tithing commitment.

That evening I realized we need to teach our kids about the blessings that come from giving our money and time—it's obviously not innate to some.

For our family, financial giving tends to be private, but we try to let our boys know about it and why we do it, so that they will hopefully be generous in their adulthood.

Our volunteer activities are more public, whether with school, church, or other organizations. We've found that our boys enjoy joining us in many of those activities—even if we sometimes have to drag them there.

If we want our kids to give freely of their time and money as adults, they need to see us joyfully doing it when they're kids, and they need to join us whenever possible.

A Driver's License
Transforms Your Family.

A new driver's license in the family is a wonderful thing. It provides a newfound independence for your son like few other life events can. It also emancipates parents by bringing a freedom to your evenings and weekends that you probably haven't had for a decade or so.

There are downsides. Your insurance payment skyrockets (and that's *before* the first accident or ticket). You have to deal with the question of whether he gets his own car, or if not, how you'll share the car(s) you already have. And at least early on, there's something new to worry about.

I remember when Rolf got his learner's permit, I let him drive my car home from the testing center. He was doing fine until he blew right through a stop sign as though it didn't exist. I pointed it out, and he said, "Oh no, I'm sorry. I think those are gonna be a problem."

After getting his license, Rolf crashed his car, Sondi's car, and my car in the course of six weeks (although only two of those cars were totaled—so there's that). He was only really at fault in one of those accidents, but we still needed to practically take out a second mortgage to pay the next insurance bill.

Despite the headaches, a driver's license is a transformational milestone for a family—mostly in a good way.

Go on a Trip with a Mission.

Mission trips can be life-changing for kids (and adults). I went on two mission trips with Rolf when he was in high school—one to the Boundary Waters Canoe Area and one to La Paz, Bolivia. In very different ways, they were amazing, and Rolf tells me they're both part of his life's highlight reel.

These trips not only gave us a chance to serve others who needed some help, but they introduced both of us to new challenges and took us out of our comfort zones in multiple ways.

For example, in the Boundary Waters, we had no cell phone coverage and no way to communicate with the rest of the world for a week. We spent part of the week at a camp, helping to clear brush and paint buildings, and spent part of the week out in the wilderness. My biggest anxiety about the trip (as it occurred just as I was beginning a campaign for governor) was being unreachable if something catastrophic happened in the race.

Rolf's biggest anxiety: pooping in the woods.

Dads and sons have different perspectives on life.

By the way, you don't have to go on a "mission trip" to experience this with your kids. Take a weekend to go somewhere fun and add an element of service in that community. Or take part of a day on a family vacation to volunteer somewhere. It doesn't matter where you go, a little research will likely yield many service options.

Take your kids on a trip with a mission component to it. You'll all remember it for the rest of your lives.

We May Never Get a Second Chance.

Most of us have the best shot at raising our kids *before* they leave us and strike out on their own. There are occasional cases where a child leaves and comes back and you have a second chance, but the prodigal son story is pretty unique.

While I hope to influence and teach my boys until the day I die, my most impactful days as a dad likely ended when they each left for college.

Make the best of every day you get with them to "raise" them right, because you may never get another chance.

Practice What You Preach.

Kids can smell hypocrisy a mile away (which is surprising for boys, since most of them can't smell themselves for a couple years during middle school).

They particularly notice when their parents are hypocritical. Sometimes hypocrisy from a parent is just fine, by the way. Adults live under different rules than kids regarding all kinds of things, and "Because I'm the dad" and "Life isn't always fair" are often perfectly acceptable answers.

But, we should always do our best to practice what we preach in matters both large and small.

Whether it's using bad language, gossiping, or making fun of someone, we lose a lot of credibility when we tell our kids to act a certain way and then don't follow our own advice.

I was on my boys *constantly* for years about leaving their dirty clothes in a pile on the bathroom floor, sometimes interrupting whatever they were doing for a walk to the bathroom to pick up after themselves. One day they turned the tables and brought me to the bathroom to highlight my workout clothes on the floor. And of course, every time I'd hound them about the issue thereafter, I heard, "But you do it too."

They're watching and listening. Practice what you preach.

It's Their Job to Embarrass Us.

I could fill a book with stories illustrating this Boy Lesson. It's just part of parenthood.

There are the cute little embarrassments that your toddler might trigger when he pulls his pants down in public. Or the more embarrassing embarrassments when they share more information than you'd like.

When Rolf was in elementary school, I used to go on an annual pheasant-hunting trip with some friends, but the trip was more about camaraderie than hunting. We'd hunt during the day and spend the evenings grilling fat steaks, drinking beer, and smoking cigars. One of our friends always brought expensive wine to drink with dinner, and we even had a hot tub out on the deck of our cabin that I'd visit in the cold fall night air before bed. Not a bad weekend.

One year, I was at the grocery store with Rolf buying food supplies for my annual hunting trip when we ran into a couple of Rolf's friend's dads, who I'd describe as the "cool" dads in our circle. One was a former NHL hockey player and the other was just one of those guys you always wanted to show up at your parties. (Yes, high school never ends.)

When they told us they were stocking up at the store for their own annual hunting weekend, Rolf chimed in that I was shopping for a hunting weekend as well, but that my hunting trips were "mostly about drinking wine and sitting in the hot tub." I assertively clarified that my hunting trips were all about killing animals and being a man, but the damage was done.

Worse yet, our kids sometimes trigger those embarrassments that other parents laugh about when they're with you but question your fitness as a parent when they're not.

Case in point: Thor has always been a rule-follower and a kind soul. I certainly never thought he was capable of being a bully. When he was in sixth grade, I was talking to a friend of mine who I hadn't seen in a couple years and had recently received our family Christmas card. He had a son a little younger than Thor, and he told me when his son saw our card, he pointed at the picture of Thor and said, "Hey, that's the kid who used to sit on me on the bus every day last year."

He laughed about it with me—and then I'm sure went home and questioned with his wife what kind of a dad would raise a kid like that.

As embarrassments often do, it prompted a great opportunity for a father-son chat.

They embarrass us—make the best of it.

Judge People By How They Act, Not How They Look.

The two greatest commandments we learn in the *New Testament* are pretty simple: love God and love people. Kids are better at the loving-people part than most adults.

Both my boys have strong convictions about many things, but like most kids, they usually look past color or religion or physical ability and judge people based on their actions. When they're little, kids see two kinds of people: those who are nice and those who are not.

It doesn't mean biases don't exist—we all know they do. But my kids' generation is better about this than mine, and mine is better than my parents'.

Having said that, I have to admit, Thor did let a hidden intolerance come to light a few years ago when he told us that, no matter how kind, engaging, and beautiful a woman might be, he would never marry a Packer fan.

Maybe some biases are okay.

Persistence Pays.

I learned this positive lesson from my boys because they so effectively used it in a negative way.

As a dad, I've worked hard to not give in to persistent whining from my sons. Sometimes, however, after the eighth plea to sleep over at someone's house or play one more game of Madden before bed or stay out an extra thirty minutes, we have a moment of weakness (and sanity-saving common sense) and just give in.

I'm not proud of that, but we all have our breaking points.

This lesson of persistence, however, can be used for good as well as evil.

When trying to land a job or an interview or a donation, asking once and then stepping back so as not to annoy someone will usually produce a predictable response—nothing. Persistence is usually needed to accomplish something of value or obtain something important to you.

One of the many valuable lessons I've learned from my boys: Being a pest once in a while can actually pay dividends.

Live for the Moment.

I'm good at letting go of the stresses of life when I'm on vacation with my family. But on a day-to-day basis, even when I'm doing something enjoyable or relaxing, the to-do list is usually somewhere in the back of my mind.

Boys can live in the moment no matter what's going on around them. That's not always ideal, as sometimes what's going on around them deserves their attention. But it's really a wonderful trait that many of us lose as we get older.

It's why little kids can be surrounded by new toys on Christmas morning and play with a box because it catches their imagination. It's how older kids can shut out absolutely everything in their environment and live in the video game they're playing or the TV show they're watching. And it's how teenagers can lose all track of time and their responsibility to respond to your texts because they're having so much fun.

It can cause parents great frustration, but it's how kids are wired. We could all use a little more of it in our own lives. Take a lesson from your children: Forget about the responsibilities of life once in a while, and just live in the moment with them.

Celebrate Their Strengths.

We are each complex and unique with different skills, passions, strengths, and weaknesses. Find your kids' strengths and celebrate them.

As a dad, I want my boys to be the best they can be, and sometimes that causes me to focus on areas that need improvement. It's important as parents to encourage our kids to improve themselves and give them guidance and correction when warranted. But we also should be constantly celebrating their strengths and helping our children develop and build on them.

We learn our kids' strengths as they grow up just through observation, but there are also many great tools out there to help identify them. One is the Clifton StrengthsFinder. It was originally designed to help adults identify their strengths in the professional world. A version for older kids is a wonderful exercise for families. The thrust of StrengthsFinder is that we should put our energy and effort into using and developing our strengths, not on addressing or overcoming our weaknesses (as is often the human default).

Whether you use a tool like StrengthsFinder or not, help your kids understand their strengths and continually celebrate and develop those strengths with them.

Learn What They Love—
No Matter How Stupid.

This one is pretty easy when your kids are little (because what they love tends to be simple and doesn't require much physical coordination or ability).

I played a lot of *Madden NFL* with my boys when they were little; helped coach their soccer, baseball, and youth football teams; played Pokémon cards with them (which I am still convinced really have no rules—just whatever little boys make up), and watched a lot of painful television (every episode of *Zoey 101* literally made me dumber; the *Wiggles* still haunt me; and if I had watched *Caillou* before we had kids, we'd still be childless).

However, once your children get older, engaging with them in things they love becomes much harder. First of all, they're less interested in your presence than they once were. And second, they're doing things that are more difficult to understand or physically pull off.

Once my boys entered their mid-teens, their music started to suck, their video games became too difficult for my middle-aged hand/eye coordination, and they were coached by guys who were actually more coordinated than the kids.

But I tried to find something in those high school years that we could share. For one of my boys, it was watching sports together (our fall Sundays for several years were all about church and football), and for the other it was being involved in our church's youth group.

Once your kids have outgrown the easy stuff, find *something* that they love, and share it with them.

Work Is Stressful for a Teenage Boy.

At some point in our adult years, work for most of us becomes just part of life. For some it's a miserable part of life, for a few it's a truly joyous part of life, and for most of us it's somewhere in between.

For a teenage boy, it's critical to have a job, as it helps him learn to work with others, cope with difficult situations, report to a boss, and schedule his time. Having a miserable or particularly unglamorous job as a teenager can lead to a greater appreciation for better jobs later in life (just as living in a dingy apartment or tiny dorm room brings appreciation for better living arrangements down the road).

While important, that first job can also be quite stressful in a way we don't understand (or recall), as many teenagers haven't encountered difficult situations without their parents around to help them react.

Thor's first real job (other than mowing lawns in the neighborhood) was in ninth grade at a big suburban movie theater. He was given a little uniform (black dress shirt and red bow tie), had a day of orientation, and then started working a few evenings a week. He told us it was going fine, but we noticed his hours started decreasing pretty quickly. After a few weeks, he was hardly working at all, and I forced the issue with him. He eventually admitted that he was not requesting any hours and unloaded about the job. "The slushy machine breaks all the time, and people yell at you. If you put too much butter on the popcorn, they yell at you. When you run out of Junior Mints, they yell at you. Dad, you just don't understand the pressure!"

Like in so many other instances, kids overreact. But as parents, we should remember that the first job can be stressful, and kids might not have the coping skills yet to deal with it. Understand that, and be patient, but insist that they work. Experiencing some level of stress and demand outside of school is good life preparation, and the satisfaction of doing a job well and being compensated for that is irreplaceable.

They're Each a Precious Gift from God.

Our children are the greatest earthly gift God gives us. They are each a masterpiece, knit together in their mother's womb, fearfully and wonderfully made.

They drive us practically insane and probably take weeks off our lives. They're self-centered, irrational, and naughty. They go through periods where they want little to do with us other than have us pay for things.

But they make our lives complete. We laugh with them (and sometimes at them), we cheer them on, and we see ourselves in them. They are our greatest responsibility in life and our biggest accomplishment. If we lost them, we would be devastated. And without them, we wouldn't be a family.

I thank God every single solitary day for my sons.

About the Author

Jeff Johnson is a graduate of Concordia College in Moorhead, Minnesota, and Georgetown University Law Center in Washington, DC. He has worked as an employment attorney at Cargill, Inc. in Minnesota and at firms in Minneapolis and Chicago and served as founder and president of his own firm, providing mediation and investigation services to employers. He's a former member of the Minnesota House of Representatives and the Hennepin County Board of Commissioners, and he founded NorthStar Neighbor, a Minnesota nonprofit matching volunteers with seniors in need. He was the Republican candidate for Minnesota governor in 2014 and 2018.

Jeff has spent much of the past thirty years learning firsthand the joys and challenges that boys can bring to an already full life. He's tutored boys in homeless shelters in Chicago, Washington, DC, and Minneapolis; coached them in baseball, football, and soccer; taught them in Sunday School and confirmation classes; and, with his wife Sondi, raised two awesome sons, Thor and Rolf, to adulthood.

Thank you for reading *Boy Lessons*. I hope you enjoyed it as much as I enjoyed writing it!

I have a favor to ask: Please leave an honest review on Amazon (or wherever you purchased the book). You can find a link at BoyLessons.org. I'll appreciate seeing your comments! Even more importantly, reviews are crucial on Amazon and other sites for raising the visibility of a book. Your feedback will really help get the word out about Boy Lessons.

Thanks!
Jeff Johnson

Made in the USA
Middletown, DE
23 November 2020